Earning the Girl Scout Daisy Petals

Updated for 2023

~

Rae Brewer

The opinions herein are solely those of the author and not endorsed by Girl Scouts of America.

Email Rae Brewer: kindredsoul65@gmail.com

Table of Contents

Preface: The World of Girl Scouting

So you've embarked on a journey through the world of Daisy Girl Scouts! Welcome! My own Girl Scout journey started when I was a child. Girl Scouts was very different back then. There wasn't a level called Daisies. I spent one year as a Brownie, three as a Junior and one as a Cadette. Unfortunately, by then, most girls had dropped out and there wasn't a troop for me to join. So I waved goodbye to scouting until, in 1992, I saw a blurb in the local newspaper stating that Girl Scouts was looking for volunteers. I remembered with fondness the 5 years I spent in scouts as a young girl. So with visions of camping and crafts dancing in my head, I called the number listed. That phone call led to a 30-year whirlwind journey as an adult volunteer that started in Nation's Capital and ended in South Florida in Summer 2022!

For much of those 30 years, I was a Troop Leader. For the first six years, I led a troop eventhough I had NO children of my own!

When I finally birthed a child, I gave up the Troop Leader position for ten years. However, during that time, I continued working exclusively with adults rather than girls.

I held many volunteer positions: Service Unit Manager, Service Unit Cookie Manager, Association Cookie Manager, Orientation Specialist, Organizer, Science Instructor, Registrar, Service Unit Treasurer, Council Program Volunteer, Gold Award Advisor, New Leader Coach. At times, I filled four or five positions at once!

Finally, when my youngest was of age, I once again became a Troop Leader…and I led Troop 10909 for fifteen years.

One year, in what must've been some type of psychotic break, I decided to start a new Daisy troop! No, crazy as it seems, I did not have a Daisy-aged child. And, yes, that meant that for a time I was the Leader of TWO troops!

Suffice it to say, I've filled a LOT of positions in Girl Scouts, including leading troops at all levels.

And now, I'd like to bring that expertise to you, a new Girl Scout Daisy Leader. My wish was to put together a volume that would guide new Leaders in their journey through earning the Daisy Girl Scout Petals. Many Troop Leaders often receive very little in the way of informative, effective training. The training that *IS* available in some areas doesn't always address the Petals in any detail. There are Flower Stories for each Petal that can be found online, but I found earning the Petals by using those stories to be quite boring. To be sure, there is also TONS of information floating around on the internet, but most Troop Leaders are VERY busy women who have not the time to slog through it all in an attempt to find ideas. So here, in one guide, is a wealth of fun, creative activities to assist you in easily achieving a plan for earning all ten Daisy Petals.

As overwhelming as it may sometimes seem, you CAN offer a fun, engaging and educational program for your Daisy scouts, without sacrificing too much of your precious time.

I welcome and look forward to your questions, comments and suggestions! Email me at: kindredsoul65@gmail.com

The Daisy Girl Scout Program Overview

These days, Daisies do just about everything that older scouts do: earn patches and badges, complete Journeys, go on fieldtrips, make crafts, sell cookies, do good things for other people, and in some Councils, they can even go on overnight camping trips.

In the beginning, the Daisy Program was only one year and they only earned the ten Daisy Petals. Then all the Program levels were adjusted and Daisies became a two-year Program. Two Financial Literacy Leaves, two Cookie Business Leaves, and three sets of Journey patches were added to the Program. The three Journeys followed pre-planned sessions found in hardcopy books. In 2017, three STEM Journeys, one Outdoor Journey, six Skill-Building Badges and three Progressive Robotics Badges were introduced. Each of the three STEM Journeys also had its own Badge and there was a Take Action Badge. Neither of the STEM or Outdoor Journeys had books. Their requirements were in the newly launched online Volunteer Toolkit.

Recently, the Daisy Program was modified again. The two Financial Literacy Leaves and the two Cookie Business Leaves have been discontinued and replaced with badges. Other new badges were also added. There are now six sets of badges which are progressive in nature. Each of these sets includes three badges, and in addition to the two Financial and the two Cookie, there are eleven more badges earned individually...for a total of 33 badges!! This does not include the badges earned in the Journeys!!

With the addition of so many badges and online Journeys, the Program can be quite confusing.

In addition, there are the:

- Journey Summit Pin that is earned after completing any three of the Journeys.
- Daisy Safety Award Pin

- My Promise My Faith Pins (one per year)

- Cookie Activity Pin (one per year)

- Global Action Patch (one per year)

- World Thinking Day Patch (one per year)

At this point, it should be noted that there are two types of "patches". The first are called Badges. They are listed in the official GS Guides (Binders) for each level. In the case of Daisies, this includes the Petals. These are EARNED and are always placed on the FRONT of the uniform. GSUSA has also approved both the "World Thinking Day" and "Global Action" badges for the front of the uniform. Both of these have requirements that change each year, depending on that year's theme.

The second type of "patches" are Participation Patches, which can also be referred to as Fun Patches. The only requirement for these, is for a scout to attend a fieldtrip or event or participate in some special activity. These are always placed on the BACK of the uniform. Fun Patches can be found at your local Girl Scout Shop or even online at various vendor sites such as: e-patchesandcrests.com or joycrest.com.

There is also a type of "hybrid patch" that stems from Patch Programs. Almost every Council has their own Patch Programs. They do have a set of requirements but they aren't Badges and they are not officially approved by GSUSA to be worn on the front of the uniform, so they always go on the BACK. Anyone can earn these patches, even if you don't belong to the sponsoring Council. You can find a Council's patch programs on their website, though it may be a little tricky. For most Councils, look on their website under "About" and then "Our Program" and either "Patch Programs" or "Council Patches".

With so many options to choose from, Leaders often find themselves overwhelmed! However, for the first year, it's easiest to just focus on the Petals.

Earning the ten Petals the first year gives the girls a strong foundation to build on the following year. If you have more meetings to fill, girls can earn that year's Global Action or World Thinking Day patch, or the Safety Award. The second year can be dedicated to completing one of the Journeys or any of the other Daisy Badges, Pins and Patches.

(Note – Girls should earn one of the two Cookie Badges and the Cookie Pin each year.)

A well-rounded Troop Calendar offers a balance of badge work, crafts, fieldtrips and service projects. Since there are ten Petals along with the Daisy Center, this can easily take up a large portion of the year, especially when adding in the GS holidays, ceremonies, as well as all the other activities that make a well-rounded troop.

Basic Girl Scout Traditions

Because the Daisy level is an introduction to Girl Scouts, there is so much basic information to learn and teach to the girls. Besides earning the Petals, girls should be taught several of the basic Girl Scout traditions:

One of the first things is the Girl Scout Sign. To do it, you hold up the first three fingers of your right hand…like the number 3, but push all three fingers close together. Girl Scouts make the Sign whenever they say the Girl Scout Promise. The three fingers symbolize the three parts of the Girl Scout Promise.

The Quiet Sign is imperative for keeping control of the meetings. Simply hold up the right hand overhead with all five fingers extended. This symbolizes the original Fifth Law of Girl Scouting: A Girl Scout is Courteous. When anyone sees the Quiet Sign, they're supposed to stop talking and raise their right hand over their head too. Soon everyone in the room will have their hands up and the room will be quiet! Girls LOVE to practice this. Have them chatter noisily for a minute or two, then pop your hand up and watch how excited they become as they race to close their mouths and raise their hands.

(Note: Oftentimes, people will raise the GS Sign overhead. This is a newer version of the Sign.)

There is also a special Girl Scout Handshake! To do it, you make the Girl Scout Sign with your right hand and shake with your left hand! The Handshake is usually only used in ceremonies.

Girls also need to learn about Juliette Gordon Low. She brought Girl Scouting to the US on March 12, 1912 in Savannah, Georgia. We celebrate March 12 every year as the Girl Scout Birthday. We also celebrate Oct 31, because it was Juliette Low's birthday. Juliette's nickname was Daisy.

There are two more special days that Girl Scouts celebrate. One is Thinking Day on Feb 22. It is a day for all Girl Scouts around the world to "think" about all the other Girl Scouts around the world. Sometimes troops have a Thinking Day event where they learn all about other countries. They might try a food from another country or play a game from another country.

The other special day is Leader Appreciation Day on April 22, sometimes called Volunteer Appreciation Day, when we celebrate and show our thanks for our Troop Leaders and Volunteers.

Daisies should also learn the Girl Scout Promise. When girls learn the Promise, they earn the blue circle patch that is the Center of the Daisy Petals.

The Friendship Circle and the Squeeze make a great closing for troop meetings. Girls stand in a circle, crossing their right arm over their left, and grasping the hands of the girls next to her. Girls often sing a song while in the circle. Then, a designated person starts the Squeeze, by GENTLY squeezing the hand of the girl next to her. That girl then "passes" the Squeeze by GENTLY squeezing the next girl's hand. In this way, the Squeeze travels around the circle to the originator. When it gets back to the beginning, girls spin to the right so that they are facing outside the circle, without dropping hands.

Be sure to stress the GENTLY part! And be prepared for the Squeeze to get "lost" at some point along the circle. Some Leaders try to prevent this by having each girl place her left foot in the center once she has received the Squeeze, which gives a visual of where the Squeeze is in its journey around the ring. This placing of the left foot also helps girls to spin the correct way.

You may choose to introduce your girls to a Kaper Chart. This is a special job chart that assigns each girl a task at each meeting. It might be taking attendance, passing out papers or leading the Girl Scout Promise. At the next meeting, each girl does a different job so all girls get a chance to do all the jobs. Kaper Charts are also used a lot at camp.

It's important to hold an Investiture Ceremony early in the scout year, typically in October. This ceremony welcomes new girls/adults into Girl Scouts for the very first time. A girl/adult is only invested ONCE in their lives! In future years, girls/adults are Rededicated. Girls/adults usually get their Girl Scout Pin at the Investiture Ceremony. There are some lovely Investiture patches available online to commemorate this special event.

One of the most important things girls do in Girl Scouts is Community Service Projects, activities where they help their community. As Daisy Scouts, these can be as simple as making cards for sick kids or old folks, shopping for food for the hungry, or making dog toys for a local animal shelter.

Many of the ideas found on the internet aren't really projects that the girls themselves do, rather they are collection drives. These are not the best projects for the girls...simply collecting things to donate somewhere. A better project is one in which the girls make or do something themselves. For example, rather than having a food drive, take the girls to the grocery store and have them pick out items to buy with their cookie profits. Use a nutrition label to explain how to find healthy foods (low sugar/fat, high fiber, few ingredients, etc) and explain the difference between perishable and nonperishable foods.

Older scouts transition into Take Action Projects. These are Community Service Projects on steroids. A Take Action Project incorporates longevity or sustainability, so that the Project continues into the future.

The Daisy Petal Overview

There are ten colorful Petals surrounding the Blue Daisy Center. Each Petal stands for a line of the Girl Scout Law. Daisies generally do not learn The Girl Scout Law, but to earn the Petals they do need to know what each line of the Law means.

Each petal has a flower friend and an optional Flower Story that can be found online. The light blue Petal is first and Lupe the Lupine teaches girls about being "Honest and Fair". For the yellow Petal, Sunny the Sunflower teaches girls about being "Friendly and Helpful". Other flowers that are in the stories are: Zinni the Zinnia (Considerate and Caring - light green), Tula the Tulip (Courageous and Strong - red), Mari the Marigold (Responsible for What I Say and Do - orange), Gloria the Morning Glory (Respect Myself and Others - purple), Gerri the Geranium (Respect Authority - dark pink), Clover (Use Resources Wisely - green), Rosie (Make the World a Better Place - light pink) and Vi the Violet (Be a Sister to Every Girl Scout - light purple).

Originally, all that needed to be done was to read the story, discuss the provided questions and then assign one of the provided activities for girls to do to practice that part of the Law. The Petal requirements have been updated a bit since the original stories came out…and this method can quickly become rather stale and boring anyway.

It's much more exciting and engaging if you mix it up a bit, incorporating fieldtrips, crafts and service projects. That's where this guide becomes invaluable. For each Petal, you'll find a plethora of ideas to inspire you. Simply pick and choose 1-2 activities to do with your troop, while explaining the meaning of each value and asking questions to ensure the girls understand. There are also some take-home ideas so girls can practice these values in their daily lives.

Honest and Fair – Lupe the Lupine – Light Blue

This Petal asks girls to know what it means to be honest, what it means to be fair and to put what they learn into practice.

Honesty is a virtue in our society, eventhough it may seem to oftentimes be lacking. Honest people not only do not lie, they also don't cheat or steal. Girls should be able to distinguish the truth from a lie, understand why honesty is important (even when no one's watching), and know what to do if they've been dishonest.

Fairness is often expected, although life isn't always fair. Girls should understand why they should follow the rules, what it means to be fair, and what to do if something is unfair.

Stories:

"I Am Honest" by Sarah Shuette
"Be Honest and Tell the Truth" by Cheri Meiners

"The Honest Woodcutter" an Aesop's Fable

"The Boy Who Cried Bigfoot!" by Scott Magoon

"Honest Mom, It Wasn't Me" by Julia Reed

"Honesty" by Margaret Snyder

"A Big Fat Enormous Lie" by Marjorie Sharmat

"Who Took the Cookies from the Cookie Jar" - Bonnie Lass

"Being Fair" by Robin Nelson

"When Is It My Turn?" by Sandra Donovan

"It's Not Fair" by Amy Rosenthal

"I Can Play Fairly" by Angela Leeper

"Fairness" by Kathryn Kyle

Games/Activities:

Relay races are a classic example of a "game" where honesty and fairness are imperative. Each team needs to stand behind the starting line and wait for their team member to cross the line before starting. Each person needs to correctly execute each part of the course. By setting up a simple course, instances of "cheating" or "fudging" will be numerous. After completing the race, gently point out where these instances occurred without singling out any one girl. One way to do this would be to ask questions, such as, "Was anyone tempted to start before their teammate crossed the line?" "Was it difficult to wait behind the line until your teammate crossed it?"

Truth or Lie is another active game. Place a picture of a smiley face or other "good" icon on one side of the room. Place a sad face or other "negative" icon on the opposite side. Girls run to the "good" side if you tell them something true (the sky is blue) or fair (taking turns) and to the "bad" side if you tell a lie (dogs can fly) or something that's unfair (cheating).

Musical Chairs, Red Light Green Light, and Mother May I? are all simple games with rules that must be followed to be fair and they give the opportunity to teach girls how to be a good loser.

Board games like "Hi Ho Cherry-O" and "Candyland" help girls learn how to play by the rules, how to lose gracefully and how to cheer for the winner.

A piñata is another easy way to illustrate fairness. When the piñata breaks open and spills out the treats, each girl grabs as much as she can. Afterwards, examine who got what and discuss whether or not the treats were distributed fairly.

Of course, sharing is a great way to demonstrate fairness. This can be easily illustrated by having girls share crayons while doing a coloring page.

Snack time provides another opportunity for fairness by dividing the snack equally. When two people share a food item, letting one cut it in half and the other choose first usually ensures fairness.

Show girls different ways to make group decisions fairly by voting, taking turns, drawing straws or flipping coins.

Guests: There are many people in the community who can speak about being honest and fair:

Coach or Gym Teacher
Police Officer

Judge or Lawyer

Bank Teller

Salesperson

Realtor

Fieldtrips: An outing to these places can make the learning come alive:

Sporting Event

Police Station

Courthouse

Bank

Crafts:

Spider Web – explain how telling lies is like weaving a web. One lie typically leads to more. If a spider's web becomes tangled it becomes a mangled mess, much like trying to keep up with one's lies. A web is also a trap for the spider's prey, as our lies can also trap us.

Cute spider web crafts can be found at:

http://blog.consumercrafts.com/kids-stuff/halloween-crafts-for-kids-webs/
Three popsicle sticks, crossed in the middle, wrapped with yarn.

http://www.sheknows.com/parenting/articles/973931/simple-halloween-spider-web-craft
Paperplate, hole-punched around edge, with yarn woven, criss-cross through the center.

Twizzlers – print out little "cards" that say "Be Honest, Don't Twist the Truth". Let girls decorate them with crayons or markers. Punch a hole in one corner and tie each one to 3 individually wrapped Twizzler licorice sticks.

"I Am Honest and Fair" Chart – simple chart that can be copied and sent home with each scout. When parents "catch" them being honest or fair, they earn a sticker. On the bottom of the sheet, under the chart, have girls draw/color a picture of what being honest and fair means to them.

I Am Honest and Fair

NAME:_____

Earn a sticker for being Honest or Fair

Friendly and Helpful – Sunny the Sunflower – Yellow

This Petal asks girls to be friendly and helpful at home, in her troop and in her community.

Friendly doesn't mean just being nice. Girls should learn how to make friends, be a friend, welcome an outsider, speak kindly, and be part of a team.

Helpful people are useful, cooperative and ready to lend a hand.

Stories:

"Best Friends for Frances" by Russell Hoban

"Amelia Bedelia Makes a Friend" by Herman Parish

"Goose Goes to the Zoo" by Laura Wall

"Can I Play Too?" by Mo Willems

"Be a Friend" by Salina Yoon

"Will You Be My Friend?" by Nancy Tafuri

"How to Be a Friend" by Laurene Brown

"Helping Is…" by Jane Buerger

"The Helpful Puppy" by Kim Zarins

"Edie is Ever So Helpful" by Sophy Hen

"The Child's World of Helping" by Jennie Davis

"Henry's Hand" by Ross McDonald

"Who's Hands are These?" by Miranda Paul

Games/Activities:

Center of Attention – have girls sit in a circle with one girl in the middle. Each girl takes turns saying something nice about the girl in the center. (Susie is smart. Katie is funny.)

Do a Good Turn Daily – print out three copies of the GS logo for each girl. In the center of each trefoil, print the words "I did a good turn." Have girls color the trefoils and cut them out. Explain that the GS Motto is "Do a Good Turn Daily" and that it means to do a good deed every day. Girls take their trefoils home and when they do a good deed, they should give one of their trefoils to the person they helped. At the next meeting, discuss what the girls did.

Color a Smile is an organization that collects completed coloring pages and sends them to senior citizens, overseas troops or anyone needing a smile. https://colorasmileorg.presencehost.net/

Guests:

Nurse or EMT

Teacher or Tutor

Librarian

Concierge

Fieldtrips:

Beach Cleanup or Park Litter Patrol

Visiting a Nursing Home (many Activity Directors will pair girls with appropriate residents)

"Bring a Friend" Ice Cream Social at a local shop

Crafts:

Friendship Bracelets can be made and given to a friend. It may be wise to have each girl make two, since many girls won't want to part with their bracelet after they make it.

Puzzle Necklaces are similar to Friendship Bracelets but use an old puzzle with pieces spray-painted a light color. A small hole is punched into each piece. Each girl gets two pieces that fit together and decorates them using permanent markers. Pieces are strung onto cordage or leather lacing. One is kept and the other given to a friend.

SWAPS are "special whatchamacallits affectionately pinned somewhere". Ideas abound online. Basically girls make these little trinkets and trade them, usually with girls from other troops. Girls can make 4-6 SWAPS and then give them to scouts in a sister troop. Your troop can visit the other troop. They can visit your meeting. Or both troops can meet at a park, for ice cream or pizza.

Hand Dusters will make you every mom's favorite. Have each girl decorate a white sock with fabric markers. They can even glue on googly eyes. Girls take them home, pull them onto their hands and help dust the house.

Door Hanger Chore Charts can also encourage girls to help out at home. Craft stores sell foam door hangers that slip over a doorknob. Have girls decorate the top of their hanger with markers, stickers or sticky gems. Give each girl five clothespins. Have them write a chore on each clothespin with a permanent marker. (Girls may need assistance with writing and spelling.) The clothespins are clipped onto one side of the door hanger. As each chore is completed, that clothespin is moved to the other side of the hanger. There are many examples of these online!

Make placemats that show girls how to set the table at home. Use posterboard cut to size. Girls can glue on a big circle for the plate, a small circle for the cup and fork, spoon and knife figures.

Helping Hand Pots – decorate flower pots and trace each girl's hand to make several "flowers". Mount the handprints on popsicle sticks. On each hand, write chores the girl can do at home. Fill pots with soil and "plant" the flowers. Parents can pick a flower for the girl to do each day.

Considerate and Caring – Zinni the Zinnia – Light Green

This Petal asks girls to be considerate and caring at home, at school and in their community.

To be considerate and caring is to live by the Golden Rule, and walk a mile in others' shoes. Girls should learn how to be thoughtful, kind, and sympathetic. They should also understand that sharing is part of caring, and how to handle situations in which someone is being inconsiderate or uncaring.

Stories:

"Consideration" by Lucia Raatma
"Dinosaurs Don't, Dinosaurs Do" by Steve Bjorkman
"Consideration" by Sarah Shuette
"You First!" by Pamela Nettleton

"Caring" by Lucia Raatma
"Caring" by Sarah Medina
"Caring" by Mary Small
"The Child's World of Caring" by Jane Moncure
"Emily's Sharing and Caring Book" by Cindy Senning

Games/Activities:

Play the Empathy Game – girls take turns selecting a card imprinted with a situation. Cards are read and girls determine how the person would feel in that situation.
http://www.momentsaday.com/empathy-game/

Play the Telephone Game to teach girls the important of listening to others.

Another game for teaching the importance of listening - Pair girls up and blindfold one girl in each pair. The other girls are Directors. The Directors must give verbal directions leading the blindfolded girls to a certain location picked out by the Leader (after blindfolds are in place).

The Art of Sharing – have girls use a variety of art materials to make a picture (pencils, crayons, markers, paint, stamps, etc). Every two minutes signal the girls to pass whatever they are using to the girl on their right. Their creations will change as they switch mediums, yet all will end up beautiful.

Make a "thank you" poster for first responders or "thank you" cards for teachers and parents.

Make PB&J sandwiches for a homeless shelter.

Guests:

Nurse

Psychologist

Hospice Worker

Animal Rescue Worker

Minister

Social Worker

Fieldtrips:

Go Christmas caroling or play games at a senior center or nursing home.

Deliver homemade cookies to a fire station.

Visit a local charitable organization to learn how they help their clients.

Visit a wildlife center that cares for injured animals that can no longer survive in the wild. Find out how they care for these animals.

Crafts:

Make Share a Care Jars – these little jars are filled with slips of paper, each of which has a task for girls to do, to show they care at home or at school. Examples are: tell your mom you love her, call a grandparent, hold the door for someone, etc.

Make bird feeders out of either pine cones, peanutbutter and seeds, or Cheerios and pipe cleaners.

Make Share the Love Buckets – similar to kids handing out Valentines…have each girl decorate a small container (small coffee can, Crystal Light box, peanutbutter jar, etc). Give girls slips of paper on which to write something nice for each of their troopmates. Girls drop their sentiments in eachother's buckets. Don't let them read the slips in their buckets until they get home!

Make Valentines for Veterans

Make Smile Cards – girls do a random act of kindness at school and leave a Smile Card behind. https://www.kindspring.org/smilecards/

42

Courageous and Strong – Tula the Tulip – Red

This Petal asks girls to find examples of courage and strength, honor courageous and strong people and practice being courageous and strong.

To be courageous is to be brave, to stand up for our beliefs and do the right thing even when no one is watching. Girls should understand that being brave does not mean being fearless, but being able to face their fears and not be deterred by them. Even saying "sorry" often takes courage! They should also recognize that courage does not mean doing foolish daredevil stunts.

Strength embodies not only physical might, but also mental fortitude. Girls should understand that anyone can be strong, no matter how small, and that healthy eating and exercise can give them strong bodies both mentally and physically.

Stories:

"Have Courage" by Cheri Meiners

"The Ride" by Kitty Griffin

"Snail and Slug" by Denys Cazet

"Courage" by Bernard Waber

"Drum Dream Girl" by Margarita Engle

"Stand Tall Molly Lou Melon" by Patty Lovell

"The Recess Queen" by Alexis O'Neill

"I Am Strong" by Susy Capozzi

"The Little Engine That Could" by Watty Piper

"Grow Strong" by Cheri Meiners

Games/Activities:

Often trying a new food takes courage! Bring in several new fruits and veggies and have a tasting.

Borrow a yoga or aerobics DVD for kids.

Crazy Eggs – boil a half dozen eggs and leave the other half raw. Number each egg and mix them up in the carton. Have each girl choose a number and guess whether the egg is cooked or raw (without touching it). Then have them hold their hand over a plate and crack the egg over their hand (as tempting as it may be to use their head…). Are they courageous enough to take the chance?

Mystery Bags – bring in several paper bags with items hidden inside. Girls must be courageous enough to stick their hands in and feel the item. Make some of the items gooey, slimy or include something icky like a toy cockroach. Use margarine containers inside the bags for wet items.

<u>Guests:</u>

Firefighter

Soldier

Someone who is blind, deaf or in a wheelchair

Exercise Instructor

Nutritionist

<u>Fieldtrips:</u>

Fire Department

Gymnastics, dance or cheer clinic

Some police departments offer a radKIDS program.

Martial arts demonstration

Crafts:

Courage Crowns – cut strips of construction paper
to fit around each girl's head. Have adults help them
write ways in which they've been courageous. Then
have them decorate their crowns before stapling the
ends together.

Supergirl Necklace – copy and cutout the Superman
"S" logo as a black and white outline, on white
cardstock. Have girls color it in. Help them write
one way they've been courageous on the back. Hole
punch and string on lacing or cordage.

Beaded Bracelets or Keychains – use letter beads and
other decorative beads to make bracelets or
keychains with messages such as: Stand Up, Stand
Strong, Speak Up, etc.

Button Pins – have girls decorate blank buttons with messages similar to those above.

Make cards for veterans, fire fighters, police officers, etc.

Invite some courageous and strong guests to a meeting where each girl brings in a dish to share.

Use troop funds to purchase boxes of Girl Scout cookies to donate to fire stations, police stations, veteran's clinics, hospitals, organizations that work with the disabled, etc.

Responsible for What I Say and Do - Mari the
Marigold – Orange

This Petal asks girls to be responsible for what they say, responsible for what they do and be responsible in their community.

To be responsible for what we say and do encourages us to make our word our bond, to keep our promises, take ownership of our words and actions, and be reliable. Responsible people make mistakes, but they take ownership of their mistake and try to make it right. Without the ability to take responsibility for our actions, it's difficult to develop self-respect or have the respect of others. Girls should understand that we should do what we say we will do and that hurtful words can't be unspoken but can cause harm to others.

Stories:

"Responsibility" by Lucia Raatma

"Responsibility" by Cynthia Roberts

"Can People Count on Me?" by Robin Nelson

"Child's World of Responsibility" by N. Pemberton

"I Am Responsible" by Sarah Shuette

"Bingo Did It" by Amber Harris

Games/Activities:

Learn phone manners.

Chore Charades – have girls act out various chores they do at home to show they are responsible.

Leave your meeting place better than you found it.

Pick up trash at your meeting place, at a park or beach. Discuss how littering is irresponsible.

Unspoken Words – have girls color a picture of Mari the Marigold. Then have them crumple it up. Flatten out the sheets and examine the wrinkles.

Explain that our words can be like the wrinkles. They can leave marks that can't be "fixed". Once our words cause hurt, they can't be unspoken.

Promise Pals – Provide each girl with a cutout of a trefoil. Pair up girls and have them each make a promise to do something before the next meeting. They can write it down or draw a picture of it on their trefoil. At the following meeting, have the partners check to see if they each followed through on their promise.

Take turns sending girls home with a stuffed animal & a list of "tasks" girls must do to take care of the animal. Parents can initial each task as the girl completes them.

Apologies – have girls role play how to make heartfelt apologies when they've done something irresponsible or hurtful to others.

<u>Guests:</u>

Librarian

Judge

Lawyer

<u>Fieldtrips:</u>

Library – taking care of books we check out and turning them in on time.

Park or beach cleanup.

Garden Center – where girls can learn how to care for marigolds.

Veterinarian – girls can learn how to care for a pet.

<u>Crafts:</u>

Troop Folders/Bags – have girls decorate a folder or tote bags. These can then be used for girls to keep track of their handouts and "go home" items. Girls need to show responsibility for bringing the folder/bag to each meeting.

Piggy Banks – have girls decorate piggy banks and take them home. Girls can do chores at home to earn coins to put in their bank. After a few months, or at the end of the year, girls can donate their funds to a charity chosen by the troop.

Plant marigolds for girls to care for.

Tons of adorable chore chart crafts can be found online.

Respect Myself and Others – Gloria the Morning Glory
– Dark Purple

This Petal asks girls to show respect for themselves, others and their community.

To respect ourselves and others, we take care of ourselves and show consideration of others. We treat ourselves and others in a dignified manner. Although respect is earned, everyone deserves a basic amount of respect until proven otherwise. Girls should understand that acting in a respectful manner reflects on them, their character, integrity and values.

Stories:

"Respect" by Kimberly Pryor

"Respect" & "Self Respect" by Lucia Raatma

"Respect" by Kathryn Kyle

"Treat Me Right" by Nancy Loewen

"Respecting Others" by Robin Nelson

"I Am Respectful" & "I Have Self-Respect" by Sarah Shuette

Games/Activities:

Egg Toss – explain how people's feelings can be as fragile as an egg, so we should treat others kindly, showing respect for their feelings.

Rolling Respect – have a sign that assigns each number on a die to a phrase, such as "I respect myself by…" or "I respect my parents by…" or "Showing respect is important because…" Girls take turns rolling a die and then completing the associated phrase.

Respect Bingo – provide each girl with a blank "bingo" card with squares in a 4x5 grid. Have girls write in each square, a way to show respect, such as: hold the door, thank mom, try new veggie, etc. Girls take their card home and attempt to get a "bingo" by doing the things on their card.

Use this website to create a take-home checklist for girls with ways they can show respect by helping endangered animals.

https://worldanimalfoundation.org/advocate/how-to-help-animals/params/post/1282604/10-ways-to-help-endangered-species

Guests:

Any healthcare professional

Fieldtrips:

Doctor's Office

Dentist's Office

Dermatologist Office – learn about skincare.

Salon – learn how to care for hair/nails.

Manners Workshop

Pick up litter at a local park or beach

Nature Center – learn how to respect the
environment

Crafts:

Tree of Good Manners – have girls trace their hand and a portion of their arm on light brown paper.

Then cut it out. This will form the trunk and branches of their tree. Have precut green paper in the shape of a treetop. Girls glue the treetop onto a piece of blue paper, towards the top of the page. Then glue their handprint onto the page with the fingers (branches) on top of the green paper. On each finger have girls write "please", "thank you", "you're welcome" and/or other words of respect. Mirrors – Glue foam frames to small mirrors. Have girls stick 2 large circles onto the top and bottom corners. Girls write on each circle, "I See Combed Hair" and "I See Clean Teeth". Girls can use other foam stickers or gems to decorate the rest of the frame.

Thank You Cards for parents, teachers, Leaders.

Golden Rule sign – have each girl paint a ruler with gold paint…or if you're brave, have them cover a ruler with gold glitter. Mount the rulers on a piece of black posterboard. Have the words "Golden

Rule" and "Treat others like you want to be treated" written on each posterboard above the ruler.

Bath Salts – have girls mix together the ingredients and fill jars to take home. Recipes abound on the internet but basically include Epsom salt, baking soda, essential oil and a carrier oil. Using these in their bath is a way to pamper themselves, or giving them as a gift shows appreciation of others.

Brown Sugar Hand Scrub – Mix brown sugar and coconut oil in a 2:1 ratio. Add vanilla.

Respect Authority – Gerri the Geranium – Dark Pink

This Petal asks girls to respect the rules at home, respect authority at school and in their town.

Respecting authority means showing esteem, honor or appreciation, and to be obedient to those placed over us, such as parents, teachers, government and police. Girls should learn who has authority and the difference between having authority and being bossy.

Stories:

"Office Buckle and Gloria" by Peggy Rathmann

"Police: Hurrying, Helping, Saving" by Patricia Hubbell

"Police Patrol" by Katherine Winkelman

"Police Officers" or "Teachers" by Julie Murray

"Hooray for Police Officers" by Elle Parkes

"Teachers Rock" by Todd Parr

"A Letter to My Teacher" by Deborah Hopkinson

"Mayor" by Jacqueline Gorman

"We Follow the Rules" by Sharon Gordon

Games/Activities:

Games with an "authority figure" such as Simon Says, Follow the Leader or Mother May I?

Learn how to properly fold the American Flag.

Have girls come up with a list of troop rules and write them on a posterboard.

Who's Rules? – Show girls pictures of various authority figures: parents, teachers, police, firefighter, mayor, umpire, etc. Read off various rules and have girls choose which figure implements or enforces the rule. For instance, raising your hand in class would be a teacher's rule; brushing teeth before bed would be a parent's rule; while not playing with matches would be not only the firefighter's rule but also parents and police!

If You Were Mayor – Write down several "rules" that a town might have on slips of paper. Examples: All buildings must be pink. Roads must have sidewalks. No cats allowed. Have each girl pick a slip and read the rule. Then have each girl draw/color a picture of the town, illustrating the rules. As a group, look at each drawing and discuss if all the rules were followed. Were all the rules "good" ones? Did some rules cause problems? Then have girls come up with rules for their town if they were mayor.

Guests:

Police Officer

Soldier

Judge

Teacher/Principal

Mayor or Government Official

Umpire/Referee

Fieldtrips:

Police Station

Town Hall

Army National Guard

Crafts

Plant geraniums to give to a teacher, or local government official. Decorate the pots.

Decorate wooden mallets/gavels or make them out of pencils pushed into corks.

Create "Wanted" posters of characters that did not respect authority.

Make cards for Operation Gratitude to send to Veterans and First Responders.
https://www.operationgratitude.com/express-your-thanks/write-letters/

Treats for the Streets – have girls decorate white lunchbags. Inside, place several treats for your local police officers: Lifesavers (for the many lives they save), Hershey Kisses (to show our love), Tootsie Rolls (to help them roll with the punches), Peppermint Patty (to help them keep their cool), Snickers (to help them keep their humor), etc. Fold down the top of each bag, punch two holes, thread a

dark blue ribbon through the holes and make a bow,
tying the bag closed. Print out a list of each candy &
its "description" and attach to each bag.

Use Resources Wisely – Clover – Dark Green

This Petal asks girls to reduce, reuse and recycle.

To use our resources wisely prompts us to be diligent in taking and using the natural assets of our world. But "resources" can also encompass money, time, energy, etc.

Stories:

"Caring for Our Air" by Carol Greene

"Saving Water" by Sharon Dalgleish

"Water Pollution" by Sean Price

"10 Things You Can Do to Save Electricity" by Jenny Mason

"Being Wasteful" by Joy Berry

"Green Mother Goose" by Jan Peck

Games/Activities:

Recycle Relay – have a pile of various recyclables and labeled boxes for each type. Split girls into teams and time how long each takes to sort the pile.

Waste No Water – Split girls into two teams, each with its own container filled to the brim with water. (Containers should be identical.) Girls must each travel down to a specific point and return, carrying their team's container. The team with the most water left at the end is the winner.

Waste-free Lunch – Bring in various reusable containers and ask girls what food items they could pack in them, instead of using throw-away materials.

Pass It On – with parent permission, have girls bring in clothes, games, books, and clothes that they no longer need and set up a time to take them to a local charity.

Guests:

Environmental Scientist
Trash Collector
Park Ranger

<u>Fieldtrips:</u>

Recycling Center

Electric Company

Water Treatment Plant

Garden Center or Nursery – learn about composting

<u>Crafts</u>

Plant seeds in cardboard egg cartons or make a terrarium out of a 2-liter bottle.

Make a bracelet out of pop tops and ribbon.

Make a pencil up out of a tin can.

Composting Jar – have each girl layer some soil, a bit of newspaper, fruit/veg peels and dead leaves/grass in a wide-mouth glass jar. Repeat the layers until jars are nearly full. Add one cup of rainwater and put the lid on. Poke some holes in the lid and draw a line marking the top of the layers. Set the jars in a sunny window and watch as nature turns the organic matter into a nutrient-rich soil in about 12 weeks.

Rain Barrel – Collect a clean, plastic coffee canister for each girl and cut out the center of the lids, leaving about a ½" border. They can be spray-painted a light color so that girls can decorate them. Take off the lid, cover the top of the canister with tulle, and replace the lid. The lid should be taped tightly to the canister using ducktape. Girls can place their rain barrels outside to collect rain for use in watering houseplants.

Make signs for girls to post in their bathrooms reminding their families to "turn off the water" while brushing their teeth.

Make the World a Better Place – Rosie the Rose – Pink

The Petal asks the girls to start with their community, protect the environment and be a changemaker.

Daisy Scouts may not think they can make the world a better place. But anytime they address a community need, no matter how small, they make an impact.

Stories:

"100 Ways to Make the World Better" by Lisa Gerry

"Amelia to Zora: 26 Women Who Changed the World" by Cynthia Chin-Lee

"She Persisted" by Chelsea Clinton

"Can We Help?" by George Ancona

"Being a Good Citizen" by Rachelle Kreisman

Games/Activities:

Filling shoeboxes for Operation Christmas Child. Have each girl bring in some items. Ideally, girls would do some chores at home to earn the money to purchase a couple items.

Pick up trash at your meeting site.

Busy Books for Children's Hospital – Purchase a few boxes of crayons and coloring books. Tear out the coloring pages. Have girls put 4 crayons into Ziploc snack bags. Each girl collects 4 coloring pages and a baggie of crayons and staples them together.

Check out: projectgivingkids.org for ideas on how to save the environment and be an advocate or changemaker.

Help girls plan a sample meatless menu their family can make for dinner.

https://www.natgeokids.com/uk/home-is-good/how-to-be-a-changemaker/

Talk about petitions. Come up with some ideas of issues the girls care about. Petitions can be about anything, like the environment, or animal welfare. Some petitions, which get lots of signatures, can be picked up by newspapers or politicians and can start the spark for change in your local area or even across the whole country!

Guests:

Local charity organizations
Peace Corps volunteer
Arborist – help girls plant a tree

Fieldtrips:

Take the troop grocery shopping with their cookie profits to purchase food to donate to a local food pantry. Girls love picking out the items they want to give to the hungry.

Collect items from the Wishlist of a local animal shelter or sanctuary and deliver them. Many will give free tours.

Visit a florist to learn what the different colors of flowers mean and how to arrange flowers.

Tour a chocolate shop or bakery and then decorate cookies or make chocolate-covered treats to donate.

Crafts

Make simple crafts from Oriental Trading Company and donate to a local nursing home, Meals on Wheels or Veteran's Clinic.

Make dog or cat toys for a local animal shelter. Simple toys can be made by tying a tennis ball or an empty 16oz water bottle in a sock, fringing the ends of toiletpaper tubes with scissors and covering with felt, or filling baby socks with catnip.

Make no-bake treats for the shelter dogs: Mix ½-cup of peanutbutter (or soybutter), ½-cup honey, 1 cup powdered milk and 1 cup rolled oats. Form the mixture into small balls and roll in ½-cup of wheat germ.

Smile Rocks – have girls draw smiley faces on those smooth pebbles used to decorate fish tanks. Girls can leave them all around town: on restaurant tables, in restrooms, on classmate's desks, on mom's pillow, etc.

Make "Turn off the light" labels for use at home.

Decorate small pots and plant herbs or sprout offcuts from lettuce or celery.

Make signs supporting a cause girls care about.

76

Be a Sister to Every GS – Vi the Violet – Light Purple

This Petal asks girls to celebrate their differences, learn about scouts around the world and support sister scouts.

To be a sister to every Girl Scout is to recognize the worldwide scouting movement as a sisterhood of like-minded girls, who strive to adhere to a set of values that create girls of courage, confidence and character.

Stories:

"Here Come the Girl Scouts" by Shana Corey
"Same, Same but Different" by Jenny Sue Kostecki-Shaw
"What if We Were All the Same?" by C. M. Harris
"The Big Umbrella" by Amy June & Juniper Bates
"It's Ok to Be Different" by Sharon Purtill

Games/Activities:

Listen to some culturally diverse music.

Try foods or play games from another country.

Have each girl talk about 1-2 of her families traditions. Do they have a special food they eat? How do they celebrate the holidays? If possible, have them bring in something from the country of their heritage.

Celebrate a holiday from a different culture.

Flat Juliette is a great way to interact with scouts anywhere in the world. Each girl is given a Flat Juliette to decorate. These are then exchanged with a troop in another state/country. Girls each take home one of the sister troop's Flats for a couple weeks. In that time, photos are taken with FJ everywhere the girls go to show what life is like in your area. Each girl can also collect some regional trinkets. The FJs, photos, and trinkets are then sent to the other troop. That troop will do the same and return your FJs with photos and trinkets from their area of the world. Find Flat Juliette all over the internet.

Learn about Girl Guides in another country. What are they called? What do their uniforms look like? Learn to say hello in that country's language. Try a food, play a game or sing a song from that country.

Assist another troop with their service project.

Assist a Senior or Ambassador scout with their Gold Award Project.

Guests:

Staff from your local GS Council

Lifetime GS Member

Older scouts in your Unit

Fieldtrips:

Meet up with another troop for ice cream or pizza or just to play at the park.

Attend a Council or Service Unit event where your troop will meet girls from other troops.

Crafts

Make SWAPS or postcards to exchange with another troop. The link below is for a group that posts exchanges of Flat Juliettes, SWAPS and postcards.

https://www.facebook.com/groups/ExchangeGSLeaderChat/

Note

It is impossible for me to address herein, all the various tidbits of information/advice that I have from my 30 years in GS. If you have questions, need further explanation or have an issue not covered in this book, please email me at: kindredsoul65@gmail.com

Made in the USA
Las Vegas, NV
04 March 2024

86701300R00049